READER'S DIGEST

BiG BOOK OF
TIME

Written by William Edmonds   Illustrations by Helen Marsden

Published by The Reader's Digest Association Limited

LONDON • NEW YORK • SYDNEY • CAPETOWN • MONTREAL

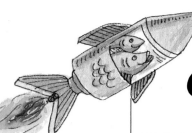

Big Book of Time

Published by
The Reader's Digest Association Limited
Berkeley Square House
Berkeley Square
London W1X 6AB

Produced by Marshall Editions

Executive Editor: Cynthia O'Brien
Editors: Kate Scarborough, Lindsay McTeague
Art Director: Branka Surla
Designer: Stefan Morris
Cover Design: John Kelly

Editorial Director: Ruth Binney
Production: Barry Baker, Janice Storr

ISBN 0 276 42143 4

Printed and bound in Italy

CONTENTS

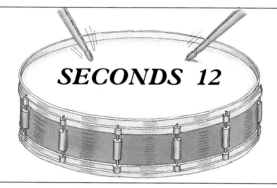

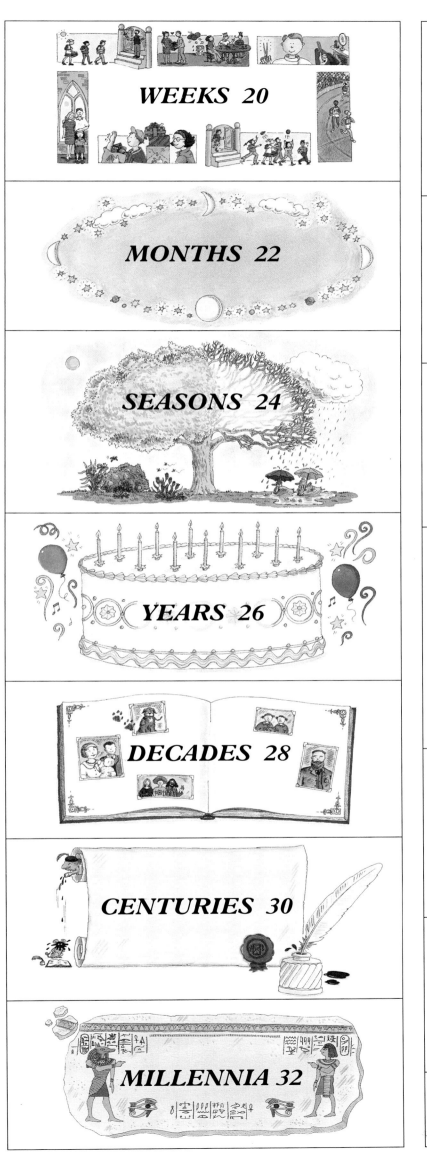
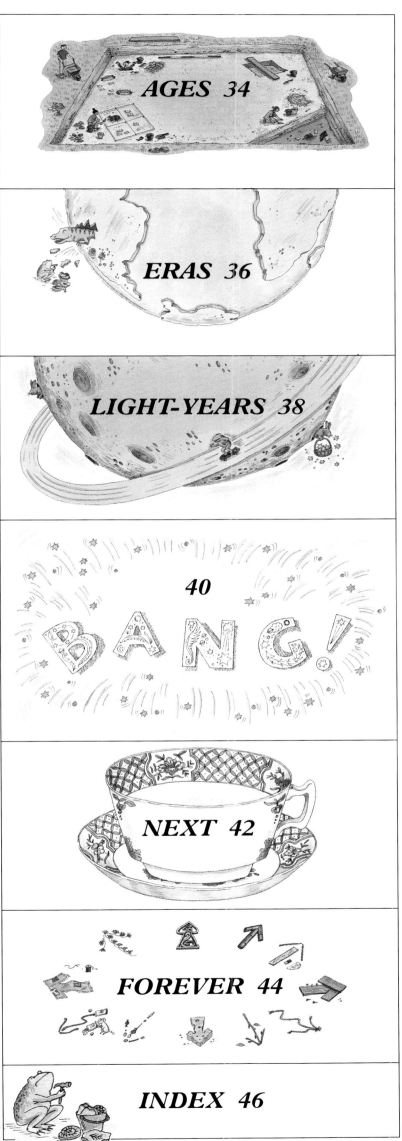

WHAT IS TIME?

Prepare yourself for a voyage of discovery. You are about to travel from the present to the dimmest distant past and into the unknown future. Search everywhere, from simply no time to absolutely all time. Look at each measure of time from the tiniest split second to the whole history of the universe. Think about what you do with time. Wonder what time does with you, and with the world and its place in space. The idea of time has fascinated people for thousands of years. It may seem to be a simple idea, but you will see it is not as simple as it seems.

6

❝ What is time? I know what it is, but if someone asks me, I am unable to tell them. **❞**

◀ That is what Saint Augustine, a wise and clever thinker, said about time 1,600 years ago. Nowadays many people still say that they have the same problem Saint Augustine had. They may know what time is but find it hard to explain or describe. In fact, time is one of the trickiest, most slippery of all ideas.

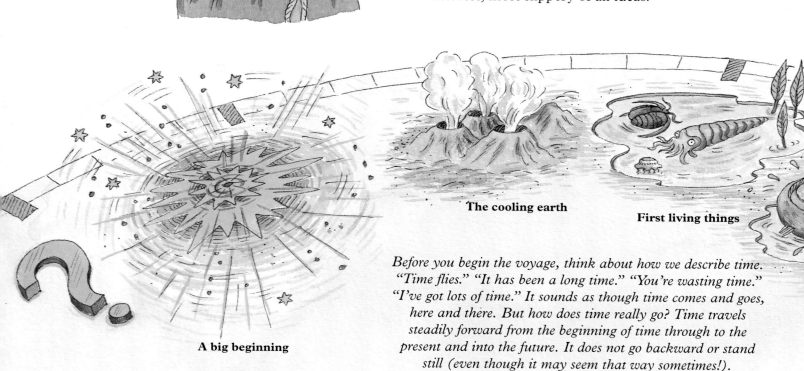

The cooling earth

First living things

Life moves onto land

Before you begin the voyage, think about how we describe time. "Time flies." "It has been a long time." "You're wasting time." "I've got lots of time." It sounds as though time comes and goes, here and there. But how does time really go? Time travels steadily forward from the beginning of time through to the present and into the future. It does not go backward or stand still (even though it may seem that way sometimes!).

A big beginning

▶ Where does time come from? Has it always existed or did people just invent it? Is it something that belongs only to us here on earth? Or is it something from outer space? What do you think?

What's the answer to this riddle?
It is always there, but you cannot see it, hear it, touch it or smell it. It points out the future, the present and the past. It is a necessity of life. It is the making of all stories. It is as long as anything takes and whenever it happens. It is the way of the world and of the whole universe.
What is it? The answer is time.

▶ Here's where the journey of discovery starts. As you learn more about time itself, you will find that time flies (that's what the Latin words *tempus fugit* mean). Climb aboard!

TEMPUS FUGIT

Dinosaurs

NO TIME
NOW

Here we are in the present! The present is now! It happens all the time in no time at all. Enjoy now, even as you read these words . . . and these words too! See how many different sides of the present you can discover, and find out just when and where now takes place.

When is now?

The time right now is exactly what any accurate clock shows. Just as the hands of a clock keep moving all the time, the present time keeps changing. You can remember the past and dream about the future, but you always live in the present.

What is now?

If you look into a mirror with another mirror behind you, you can see a reflection of yourself, and a reflection of the reflection, and a reflection of the reflection of the reflection. In fact, it may seem as though there is no end to the images. Which one is exactly now? All the reflections you see are now! The present is ongoing.

▼ The present time is not always what it seems. Look up into the night sky. The light coming to earth from the nearest star takes about 4¼ years to reach us. So we are really looking at the past. Even the light from the sun takes eight minutes to reach us here on earth.

No time to lose!
Time goes on and on like this train on a circular track. This is why it is important to seize opportunities when they arise. The saying "There is no time like the present" means that if you see a chance now to do something worthwhile, you should take it immediately. Act now before it's too late. The present opportunity is precious. You are wise to make the most of it before it disappears into the past.

Where is now?
The present lies between the past and the future. Imagine a craft floating down a river. The craft is now, gently drifting toward the future and away from the past. The craft keeps moving with the flow of the water, but always stays in the present.

PAST   FUTURE

TEMPUS FUGIT

The journey through time takes us back to the past, forward to the future, and away to for ever...

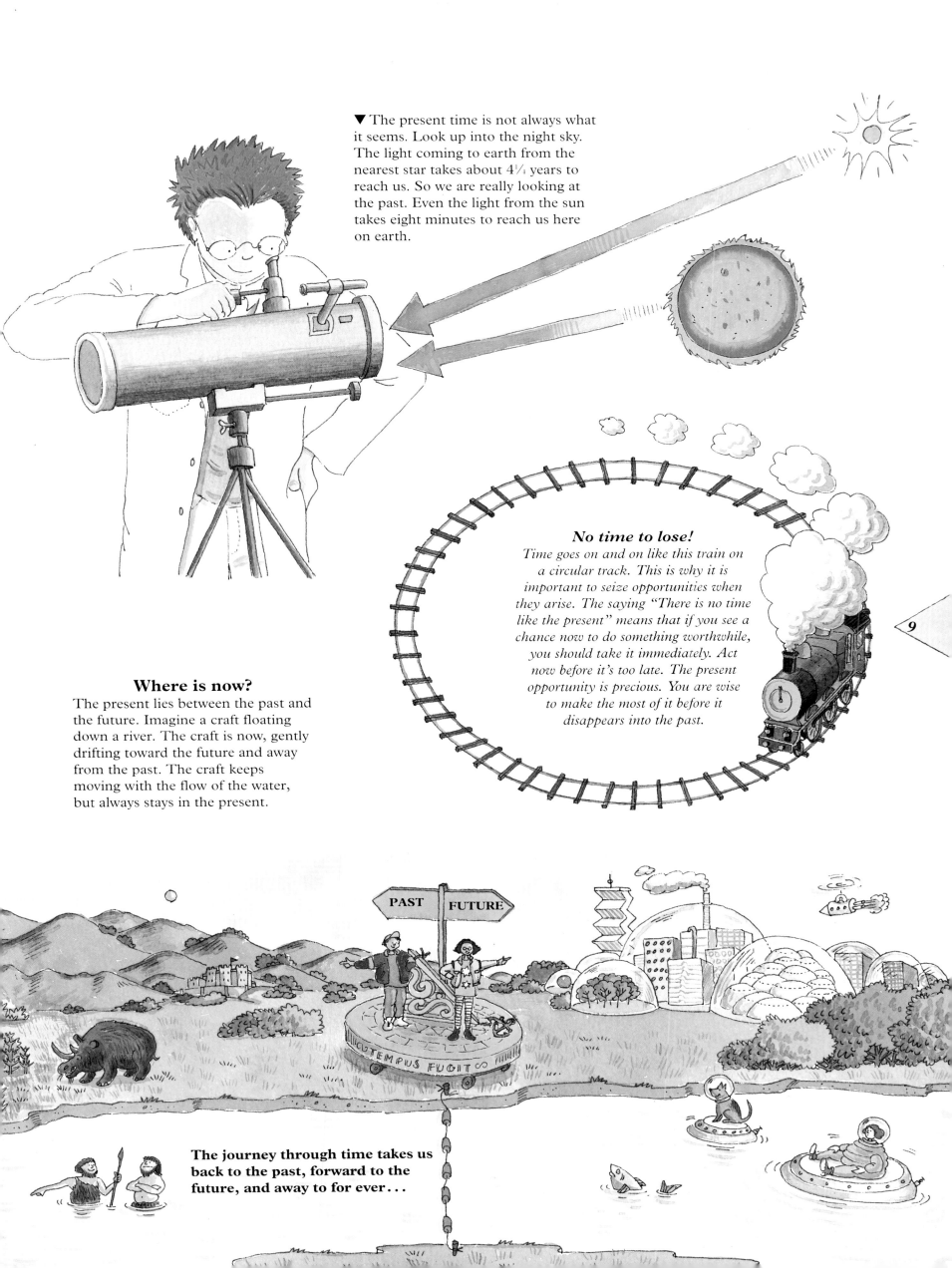

FLEETING TIME
MOMENTS

Flash! The camera captures a single moment. The moment happens so quickly, in a split second, that you can miss it completely in a blink of your eyes. Your body signals the passing of moments in many different ways. In only a moment your wink, or smile, or nod or nudge can be noticed by someone special. An athlete can win or lose a race by a mere moment. A scientist can measure an experiment in the briefest of moments (trillionths of a second). Moments come and go at lightning speed.

▼ People who make computer programs deal with timing in nanoseconds (billionths of a second). Their programs include all the information and possible choices needed to solve a problem. You may need only to push a button to tell the computer to apply the program. After just a moment the answer will appear on the screen.

Momentous moments

Some moments we never forget, whether we want to or not. All through our lives we experience moments of success, disappointment, terror and surprise!

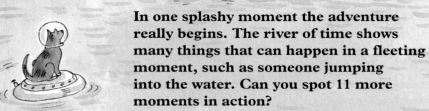

In one splashy moment the adventure really begins. The river of time shows many things that can happen in a fleeting moment, such as someone jumping into the water. Can you spot 11 more moments in action?

◀ Is it possible to hold on to a moment? Well, almost. People take photographs to capture special moments. The shutter of the camera opens, and the flash lights up for a moment—just long enough to take the picture. Then the shutter closes again. Looking at the photograph later and having it to keep is a wonderful way to remember the moment when it was taken.

▼ Lightning happens so quickly, if you blink you could miss seeing it. The power of lightning at the moment it strikes can split a tree.

Do ideas come in a moment?

Have you ever had a brilliant idea that came to your mind in an instant? Great ideas, or flashes of inspiration, often come at the most unexpected moments—even when you're in the bath. A great idea at an inconvenient moment is better than no idea at all!

▶ When does one moment end and another begin? Do they join neatly in a line, with one moment following straight into the next one? A cinema film seems to show this by capturing moments frame by frame. But when the film is run, all the moments seem to melt into constantly flowing movement.

BEATING TIME
SECONDS

Watch a clock to see the rhythmic seconds tick away. Seconds get their name because they are the second fraction (or part) of an hour. The first fraction is a minute. Sixty seconds make up a minute, 3,600 seconds make up an hour and 86,400 seconds make up a complete day and night. People love to listen, count, swing, dance or march to beats as rhythmic as the ticking of seconds.

12

▼ Tiny quartz crystals, as small as grains of sand, quake at over 100,000 vibrations a second. We can't feel this, but a microchip and a little electric battery can. They pick up these superfast beats and use them to show very accurately the passing of seconds, minutes and hours. This is how digital watches work.

▶ Old-fashioned clocks have swinging pendulums that constantly move to and fro. Each swing marks time going by. Depending on the size of the pendulum, it may swing once every second.

All these things can take about a second: a footstep, a swing, a skip, hop and dance. What can you do in a second?

Can you feel your pulse?

Your heart pumps blood around your body in regular beats. The jagged line above shows how your heartbeat would look if a doctor measured it with a special machine. Feel your heartbeat, or pulse, on the inside of your wrist. Count the beats while watching the seconds tick on a clock. The heart normally beats a little more than once every second. Jump up and down and then check your pulse again. Do you notice a difference?

What are these mice doing?

These mice represent musical notes. Each one is a separate note with one beat, except for the white mouse, which counts as two beats. Each beat could last a second, or there could be two beats to a second, or three or four. It all depends on how slow or fast the music goes.

Counting Seconds

One clap clap, two clap clap, three clap clap and on. To measure how long a second lasts, you can count it and add two claps of your hands. You can also count seconds by saying, "one Mississippi, two Mississippi, . . ." and so on. Counting out loud is a good way of showing how time passes.

drip

drip

▶ When a tap leaks one droplet a second, it takes only a minute to drive you crazy!

drip

MINUTES

Spare a minute! Find a stopwatch or a watch with a second hand and wait for the hand to go all the way around—a minute has gone by! One minute makes up a tiny, or minute, measured part of time. It is longer than a second, as you've discovered. It takes 60 seconds to make one minute, and 60 minutes make an hour. If it only takes a minute to eat a small slice of the cheesecake above, how long would it take to finish all 60 slices? And how do you think you'd feel?

How many minutes?

How many minutes do you need to do things? Two minutes to dry yourself after a bath? Five minutes to slurp up a milk shake? How about a good long 20 minutes to savour a delicious meal?

This athlete can run 400 metres.

The turtle moves about one metre.

This race measures how far these racers can go in one minute. Time your own race. How about you?

1 minute

14

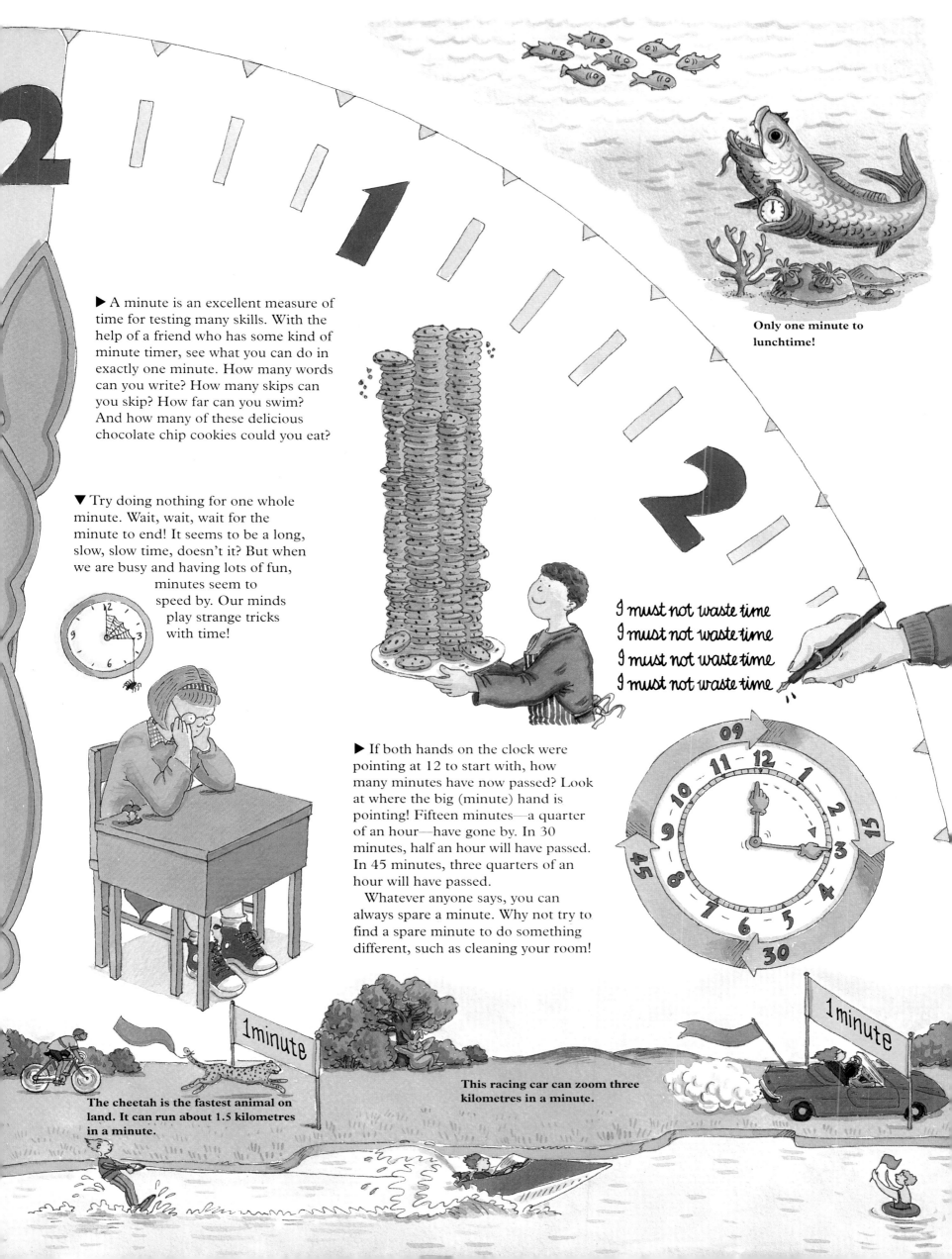

Only one minute to lunchtime!

▶ A minute is an excellent measure of time for testing many skills. With the help of a friend who has some kind of minute timer, see what you can do in exactly one minute. How many words can you write? How many skips can you skip? How far can you swim? And how many of these delicious chocolate chip cookies could you eat?

▼ Try doing nothing for one whole minute. Wait, wait, wait for the minute to end! It seems to be a long, slow, slow time, doesn't it? But when we are busy and having lots of fun, minutes seem to speed by. Our minds play strange tricks with time!

I must not waste time
I must not waste time
I must not waste time
I must not waste time

▶ If both hands on the clock were pointing at 12 to start with, how many minutes have now passed? Look at where the big (minute) hand is pointing! Fifteen minutes—a quarter of an hour—have gone by. In 30 minutes, half an hour will have passed. In 45 minutes, three quarters of an hour will have passed.

Whatever anyone says, you can always spare a minute. Why not try to find a spare minute to do something different, such as cleaning your room!

1minute

The cheetah is the fastest animal on land. It can run about 1.5 kilometres in a minute.

This racing car can zoom three kilometres in a minute.

1minute

KEEPING TIME
HOURS

When the alarm clock rings, it may be time to get up, to catch the bus, to eat a meal or to watch a favourite programme on TV. We know each hour marks the passing of 60 minutes. But it took people in history a long time to learn to keep accurate time. For example, the Egyptians learned to measure out parts of the night and day into hours by observing the changing positions of the sun. Of course, this works only if it's sunny!

The Roman numerals on the clock (above) might look funny to us because we're used to seeing Arabic numerals in their place. But Roman numerals were used in ancient Rome, and many clocks, old and new, still use them. Can you work out which number each Roman numeral on the clock represents?

▶ The ancient Chinese burned incense sticks as a way of telling the time. Some of these incense clocks changed their smell throughout the day. People could tell the hour by smelling!

◀ Water clocks marked the passing of hours by the changing level of water as it flowed out of a container. This complicated Chinese version used a waterwheel to drive the water through the mechanism of the clock.

Each of these activities takes 15 minutes. By the time you have travelled this stretch of river an hour will have passed. Time an hour of your day and see what you do with it.

How do we measure 24 hours?

Mechanical clocks, with faces something like this, were first invented more than 600 years ago. At first they were not very reliable, but gradually they became more accurate, especially with the introduction of the clock pendulum over 300 years ago. Notice that all 24 hours are marked on the clock.

▲ After a few hours without food, our stomachs rumble—we need to eat. After a few more hours we get tired and fall asleep. We eat, sleep, go to school and play. We use hours to help us keep track of our time. Our bodies get used to keeping regular hours. They can tell when it is time for dinner or time for bed, and they let us know!

▲ As mechanical clocks became more accurate, people added them to church towers and town halls. Then everybody in town told the time by the same clock. Now digital clocks on hoardings or modern buildings show the passing hours and sometimes the temperature. Most people also wear their own private clocks—commonly called wristwatches!

Today's Timetable

8:00	Wake up; have breakfast
9:00	School
10:00	English
11:00	History
12:00	PE—swimming
1:00	Lunch
2:00	Maths
3:00	School's over
4:00	Football practice
5:00	Eat dinner
6:00	Do homework
7:00	Finish homework
8:00	Watch TV
9:00	Have a bath
10:00	Go to bed

What do you do each hour of the day?

Make your own daily schedule. Your timetable might include going to school, doing chores at home and watching TV later on in the evening.

NIGHTS & DAYS

Good day! Good night! Round and round the world spins, through the light of day, the dark of night, and into daylight again, time after time. We have daytime when our side of the world is facing the sun, and night-time when our side of the world turns away from the sun's light. A complete turnaround of the world takes time—24 hours for each full spin. You can tell that the earth is spinning by watching the position of the sun and the stars.

NORTH AMERICA

4:00 A.M.

New York

5:00 A.M.

6:00 A.M.

7:00 A.M.

8:00 A.M.

SOUTH AMERICA

◀ If you ran in circles around the North Pole or the South Pole you could run faster than the earth is spinning. But that doesn't mean you would quickly run through days and nights, go into the future, or become rapidly older.

▶ Time marked A.M. begins with midnight and continues for 12 hours. A.M. stands for *ante meridiem* meaning "before noon". P.M. (*post meridiem*) time begins at noon. The world is divided into time zones. The starting point is the prime meridian, at 0 degrees longitude. A.M. and P.M. fall on either side of it.

24:00 1:00 2:00 3:00 4:00 5:00 6:00 7:00 8:00 9:00 10:00 11:00

A full day and night is made up of all the things you do from when you wake up one morning until you wake up the next morning. What makes up your day and night?

18

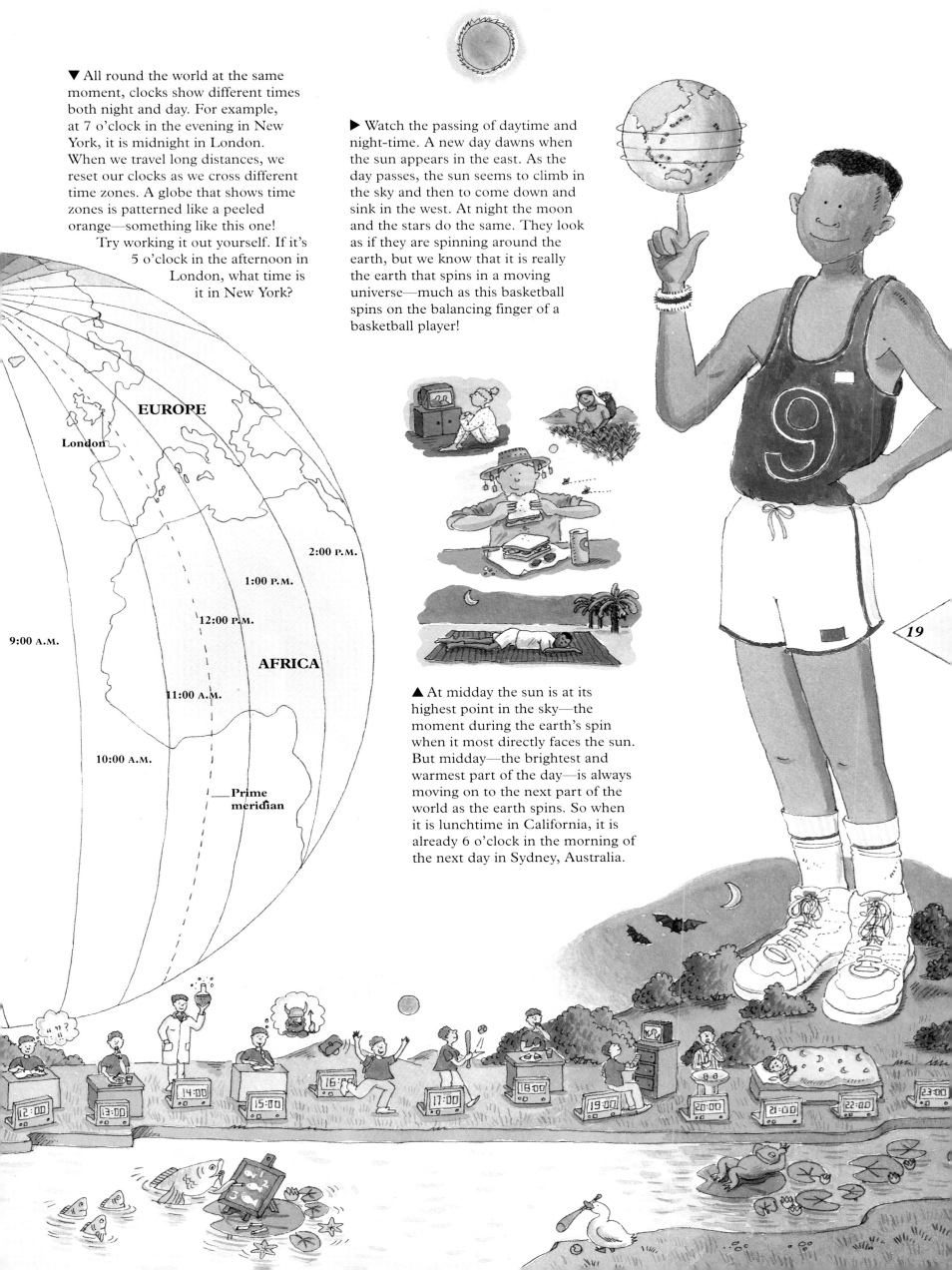

▼ All round the world at the same moment, clocks show different times both night and day. For example, at 7 o'clock in the evening in New York, it is midnight in London. When we travel long distances, we reset our clocks as we cross different time zones. A globe that shows time zones is patterned like a peeled orange—something like this one!

Try working it out yourself. If it's 5 o'clock in the afternoon in London, what time is it in New York?

▶ Watch the passing of daytime and night-time. A new day dawns when the sun appears in the east. As the day passes, the sun seems to climb in the sky and then to come down and sink in the west. At night the moon and the stars do the same. They look as if they are spinning around the earth, but we know that it is really the earth that spins in a moving universe—much as this basketball spins on the balancing finger of a basketball player!

EUROPE

London

2:00 P.M.

1:00 P.M.

12:00 P.M.

9:00 A.M.

AFRICA

11:00 A.M.

10:00 A.M.

Prime meridian

▲ At midday the sun is at its highest point in the sky—the moment during the earth's spin when it most directly faces the sun. But midday—the brightest and warmest part of the day—is always moving on to the next part of the world as the earth spins. So when it is lunchtime in California, it is already 6 o'clock in the morning of the next day in Sydney, Australia.

12:00   13:00   14:00   15:00   16:00   17:00   18:00   19:00   20:00   21:00   22:00   23:00

MAKING TIME

WEEKS

Seven days and seven nights. That's what a week **is. And four weeks, plus a day or so, make up a month.** Because days are arranged into set patterns, people like to plan their week, with certain things to do on particular days. Special days become a part of this plan: a day or two to rest from work, perhaps a special day for religious worship and a day for shopping or going to the park, or for sporting events. And how do we name these special days? In many languages of the world, day names are taken from the sun, the moon, the world and its elements, the planets or the gods.

Why seven?
The beginning of the Bible describes God creating the world in six days and resting on the seventh. The Babylonians began to use the seven-day week nearly 3,000 years ago. The seven-day phases of the moon held a mystery and magic for them. Each of these phases—from new moon to half moon, from half moon to full, from full moon to half, and from half moon to new—take just over seven days.

Monday

Tuesday

Wednesday

Here, each day of the week is marked by an activity. What do you do on each day of the week to make it different from other days?

◀ After the French Revolution of 1789, the French decided to change their calendar to 10 days in a week and to alter all the names of the months as well. Since the countries around France continued to use the seven-day calendar, communication became very difficult. So the 10-day calendar didn't last very long!

▼ In 1929 the Russians tried a five-day week. Instead of names, the days of the week had colours (yellow, orange, red, purple and green) and numbers. Each person was told which day (colour and number) was his or her day of rest. Friends could see each other only if they had the same colour and number. This led to lots of confusion, so in 1940 the calendar was changed back to the original seven-day week.

Days of the Week

Sunday (English) dimanche (French) domenica (Italian)	The Lord's day—observed by Christians as a day of rest and worship. The day gets its name from the sun.
Monday (English) lundi (French) lunedì (Italian)	The first day of our working week, named by the Romans after the moon.
Tuesday (English) mardi (French) martedì (Italian)	The English name is from the Anglo-Saxon war god, Tiw; the French and Italian names come from the planet Mars.
Wednesday (English) mercredi (French) mercoledì (Italian)	Woden is the Anglo-Saxon god who is remembered on this day. The French and Italian names are derived from the planet Mercury.
Thursday (English) jeudi (French) giovedì (Italian)	The thunder of Thor inspires Thursday. The French and Italians have taken their names from the Roman god Jove and the planet Jupiter.
Friday (English) vendredi (French) venerdì (Italian)	The Muslims' holy day, el Jumah. Our Friday is named after Frigg, the Nordic goddess of love, while the French and Italian names are derived from Venus, the Roman goddess of love.
Saturday (English) samedi (French) sabato (Italian)	This is the Jewish holy day. The planet Saturn is associated with this day.

21

▲ Imagine how confusing it would be if we had names for all the days in the year! Names for the seven days that make up the week are quite enough.

MONTHS

Watch the moon first appear and grow rounder (wax) and then become smaller (wane). As we watch the moon during a month it seems to change its shape. It goes from a crescent to a half moon, on to a full moon, and back again. The time the moon takes to complete its phases (from new moon to new moon) is called a lunar month. This is the time it takes the moon to orbit around the earth—about 29½ days. That's approximately four weeks to a lunar month, with 1½ days left over. Luckily, the Romans came up with a 12-month calendar that makes an accurate year by adding extra days to each month.

22

▶ People called astronomers study the moon, the planets and the stars.

◀ The moon does not only give us lunar months—as the earth spins we notice that its oceans fall and rise in ebb tides and flow tides. The water on the side of the earth facing the moon is pulled toward it, no matter how much of the moon is visible. High tides happen about every 12½ hours, or nearly an hour later each day.

Moon lighting
The sun lights up one side of the moon, just as it does one side of the earth. But as the moon travels around the earth, we see different amounts of the lighted side. This creates what we see as the changing shapes, which we call the moon's phases, during a month. We can't see the unlighted part of the moon, but it is still there!

In the four weeks and two or three days that make up a month, you can do many things—paint a picture or build a treehouse, perhaps. What sorts of things make up your month?

Week 1

Week 2

▶ Years ago it might have taken a month to sail across the ocean from one continent to another. Today you could fly around the world many times in one month!

January *31 days named after Janus, a two-faced Roman god.*

February *28 days named after Februs, a Roman festival to do with cleaning and purifying.*

March *31 days named after Mars, the Roman god of war.*

April *30 days from the Latin word aprilis associated with the goddess Venus.*

May *31 days named after Maia, the mythological mother of Mercury.*

June *30 days named after Juno, a Roman goddess of marriage.*

July *31 days named after Julius Caesar, a Roman general and statesman.*

August *31 days named after Augustus, the first Roman emperor.*

September *30 days from the Latin for seven, septem, originally the Roman seventh month.*

◀ To discover how many days make up each month, count with your fingers and the spaces between, but skip your thumb. Call your index finger January, the space beside it February and so on. When you reach July, go back to your index finger for August. All the finger months have 31 days. All the months that fall in the spaces have 30 (except February). A handy rhyme can also help you to remember: "Thirty days hath September, April, June and November. All the rest have 31 except February alone, which has 28 days clear and 29 in each leap year." Can you remember this?

October *31 days from the Latin for eight, octo, originally the Roman eighth month.*

November *30 days from the Latin for nine, novem, originally the Roman ninth month.*

December *31 days from the Latin for ten, decem, originally the Roman 10th month.*

How was the calendar fixed?

Months make awkward time measures because our time measures do not fit together neatly. Whole days don't fit exactly into a lunar month, nor do they fit exactly into a year, as measured by the earth's trip around the sun (which takes 365¼ days). And 365 is a difficult number to divide equally—you can only do it with 5 and 73. The Romans first tried four months to a calendar year, but this didn't work so they added six more months. Uuma Pompilius added two more, creating the year as we know it.

▲ Each of the 12 months has its own name. These names help us to mark the changing seasons and to celebrate anniversaries. In which month do you celebrate your birthday?

Week 3

Week 4

CHANGING TIME
SEASONS

Seasons! They are the signs of changing time, a way of marking time through the year. Many of us know the four seasons: spring, summer, autumn and winter. But hot countries near the equator have only wet and dry seasons. The four seasons may be divided roughly into three months each, a cycle of seasons through the year caused by the changing tilt of the earth toward the sun. Let your mind enjoy the changing seasons. Journey from spring to summer to autumn to winter, and back again to spring. The cycle of the seasons goes on and on.

▼ On its yearly journey around the sun, the earth tilts and spins, making different parts of the globe warmer or cooler depending on how close they are to the sun.

Seasons bring lots of changes. Look at the trees for signs of new leaves in spring. Enjoy the warmth of summer, the colours of autumn and the fun of winter snow.

How are the seasons celebrated?

Countries and local places around the world have special festivals that follow the seasons. Sometimes festivals mark the changing weather. Sometimes they celebrate religious occasions—holy days such as Christmas that have become holidays. But when it is summer in Australia, it is winter in North America and Europe. So Australians might go to the beach at Christmas while Canadians are huddled around the fire!

Spring and new life

It's time to welcome warmer weather, plants in bloom, hatching eggs and newborn animals. Christians celebrate Easter, rejoicing at the resurrection of Jesus Christ from the dead. Jews celebrate Passover, giving thanks for their escape from slavery in Egypt long ago.

Summer glory

Time for long holidays, outdoor fun and entertainment. Local communities enjoy summer fairs. Countries celebrate National Days. The 4th of July is Independence Day in the United States. The 26th of January is Australia Day.

Midwinter feasting

Now is the time for food, laughter and generosity. In December there is the preparation for Christmas and rejoicing to celebrate the birth of Jesus. During this time families come together and enjoy the warmth of giving and spending time with one another. Together they usher in the New Year. This celebration marks a new beginning—a chance to make new plans and to look forward to all the things to come. People welcome the New Year with balloons and parties.

Fasting

Preparing for feasts to come is an important part of celebrations. Fasting is one way that people prepare for feasts. This means giving up certain food and drink for a particular period of time. Muslims observe Ramadan in the ninth month of the Muslim year—a month of fasting before the feast of Id al-Fitr.

Autumn thanksgiving

Harvest festivals are celebrated around the world. In Canada, Thanksgiving Day comes in October; in the United States it occurs in November. In Japan people celebrate Labour Thanksgiving Day on the 23rd of November.

25

Lighting up the dark

When nights grow longer, let's light up the evening sky. Hindus celebrate Diwali, a festival of lights, between October and November. British people celebrate Guy Fawkes on the 5th of November with fireworks. In mid-autumn Chinese people light their homes to celebrate the Moon Festival.

TIME AND AGAIN
YEARS

Happy New Year! Many happy returns to Planet Earth as it completes another orbit of the sun. Celebrate the year—it is made up of 365 days (and a quarter), 12 months, 52 weeks (and a day), 8,766 hours or 525,960 minutes. The earth takes a little longer than 365 days to orbit the sun. Every four years this adds up to an extra day, so every fourth year is a leap year with one extra day, the 29th of February. Each year, special days such as birthdays, religious feast days and national holidays return.

We use years as markers to keep track of anniversaries, how old we are or how old our country is. Look back over the past year of your own life. See how years can teach you new things. What will you learn this year?

◄ Each planet moving around the sun takes a different time to complete its orbit. Mercury, the planet nearest the sun, takes about 88 earth days to complete an orbit. Pluto, the planet farthest from the sun, takes about 248 earth years to complete an orbit.

The year is made up of 12 months. In which month is your birthday?

January *February* *March* *April* *May* *June* *July*

What is New Year's Day?

It's always fun to welcome a new year. Throughout much of the world, people mark the start of a new year on the first day of January (which is midwinter in the northern half of the world and midsummer in the southern half). Some cultures mark the yearly cycle at other times. The Chinese celebrate New Year festivities about three to four weeks after the 1st of January. The Jewish calendar marks the New Year in September. How and when do you celebrate New Year?

▶ Each year you grow a little taller and a little stronger, until you're about 20 years old. Measure your height now. How tall do you think you'll be a year from now? Just think about how much you've learned and grown in the years since you were very small!

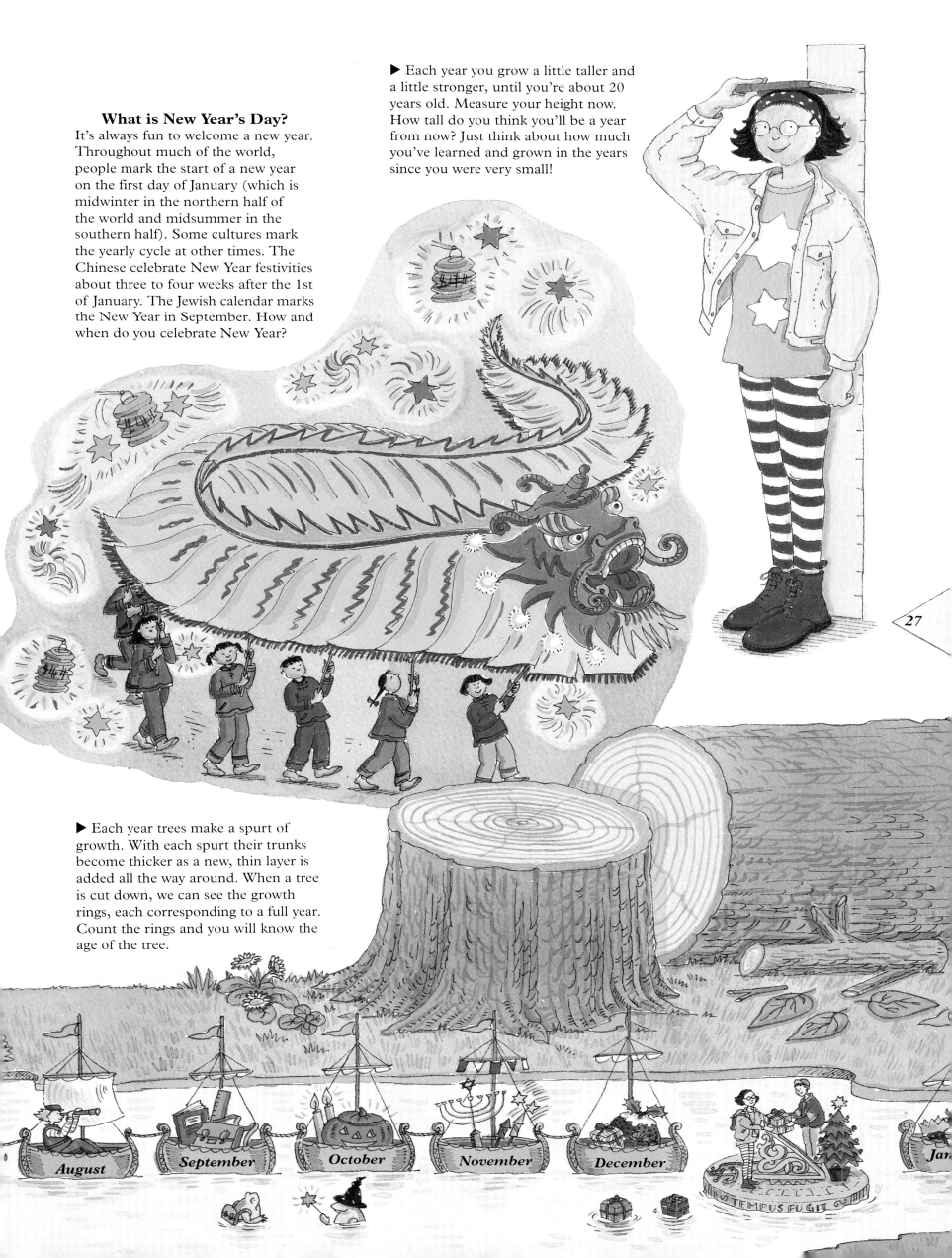

27

▶ Each year trees make a spurt of growth. With each spurt their trunks become thicker as a new, thin layer is added all the way around. When a tree is cut down, we can see the growth rings, each corresponding to a full year. Count the rings and you will know the age of the tree.

August *September* *October* *November* *December* *Jan*

TEMPUS FUGIT

TIME LIVED
DECADES

A **decade is 10 years. Your lifetime will probably last many decades.** You will grow up through your first decade into your teens, then change in many different ways as you live through your twenties, thirties and so on—maybe even into your eighties or nineties. Compared to most other animals, this is a long life span. Unlike those other animals, your memory and imagination allow you to think back over decades that have passed. You can also plan and dream about all the decades to come.

▲ Average life spans of different animals vary greatly. Elephants can live for eight decades, ostriches for six and parrots for five. How many decades do toads live? Wolves? What about robins? A shrew usually lives for just one-tenth of a decade—only one year.

◀ Bigger animals usually live for a longer time than smaller animals, but not always. Elephants are much bigger than humans but live up to eight decades, the same as a human being with a good, long life.

400cm
13ft.

350cm
11½ft.

300cm
10ft.

250cm
8¾ft.

200cm
6½ft.

150cm
5ft.

100cm
3¼ft.

50cm
1½ft.

0

Look at all you learn in the first 10 years—the first decade—of life.

Crawling

Walking

Talking

Climbing

Building

Going to school

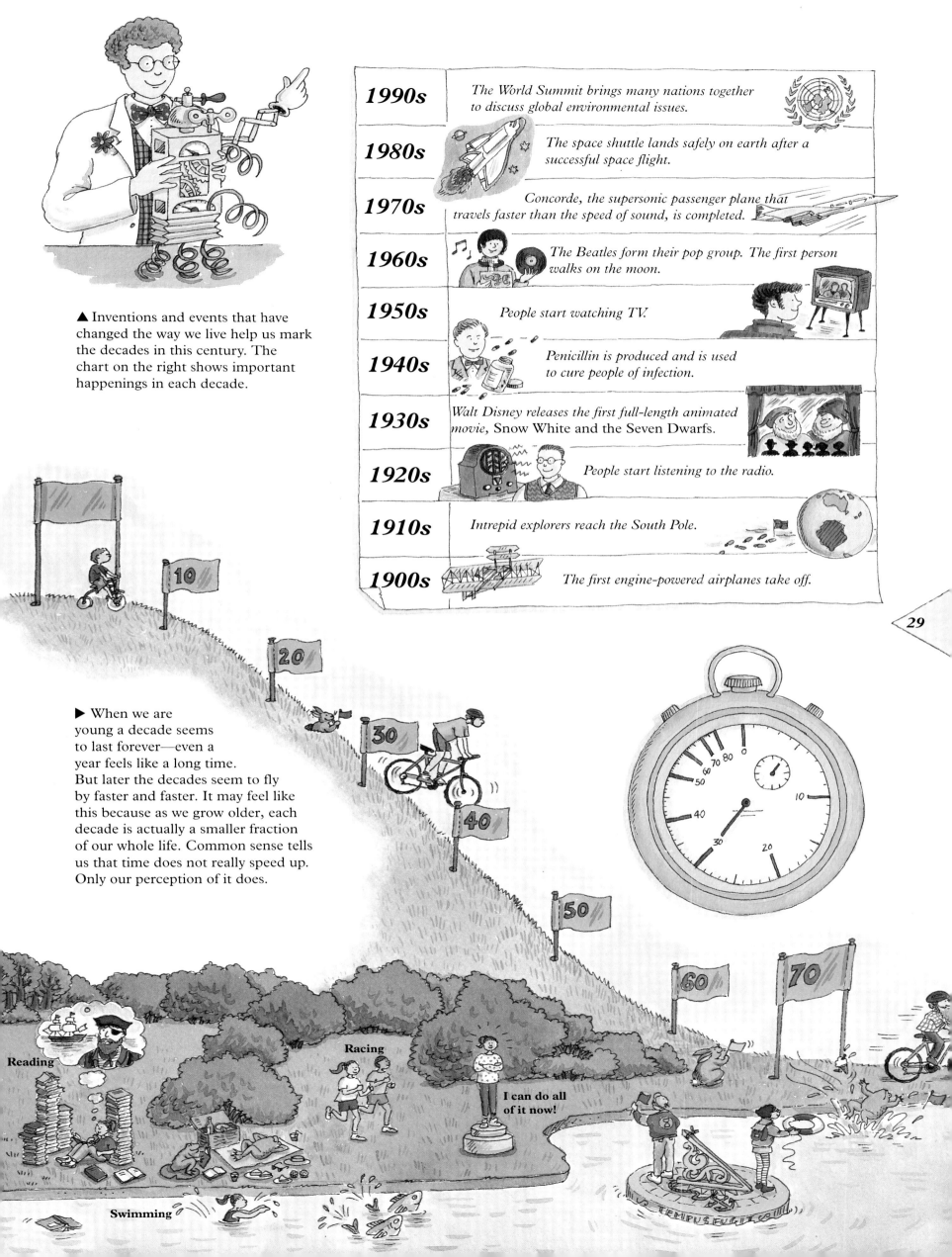

▲ Inventions and events that have changed the way we live help us mark the decades in this century. The chart on the right shows important happenings in each decade.

1990s	The World Summit brings many nations together to discuss global environmental issues.
1980s	The space shuttle lands safely on earth after a successful space flight.
1970s	Concorde, the supersonic passenger plane that travels faster than the speed of sound, is completed.
1960s	The Beatles form their pop group. The first person walks on the moon.
1950s	People start watching TV.
1940s	Penicillin is produced and is used to cure people of infection.
1930s	Walt Disney releases the first full-length animated movie, Snow White and the Seven Dwarfs.
1920s	People start listening to the radio.
1910s	Intrepid explorers reach the South Pole.
1900s	The first engine-powered airplanes take off.

▶ When we are young a decade seems to last forever—even a year feels like a long time. But later the decades seem to fly by faster and faster. It may feel like this because as we grow older, each decade is actually a smaller fraction of our whole life. Common sense tells us that time does not really speed up. Only our perception of it does.

Reading

Racing

I can do all of it now!

Swimming

TIME RECORDED
CENTURIES

Centuries see the unfolding of history. Each century equals 10 decades, or 100 years. You learn about the passing of centuries mainly by reading what has been recorded—in books, diaries, reports and all kinds of documents. Every century of history is made up of many stories about people, their homes, their countries and the changes they experience. History also tells how people over the centuries adapt their way of living with time itself, using ever-changing ways of keeping records, travelling and communicating.

30

▲ Photography came about in the 19th century (the 1800s). The first negative photograph was taken in 1835 by William Henry Fox Talbot. This paved the way for the widespread making of accurate pictorial records with photographs, films and video recordings.

▶ Printing was invented in the Far East. The first known printed book, the *Diamond Sutra* from China, was made with wooden blocks in AD 868. Six centuries later a new method using separate metal parts for each letter (movable type) was introduced by Johannes Gutenberg in Germany. After that, printing became a big industry all over Europe.

The river of time shows a century of cars and a century of changes in bathing suits.

1990 1980 1970 1960 1950

Pendulum clock–17th century

Sundial–3000 BC

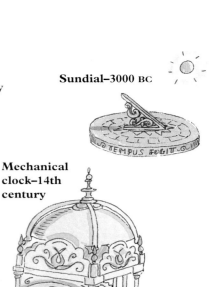

Mechanical clock–14th century

Ship's clock–18th century

How have the centuries changed our lives?

Seeing the different timepieces people have used over the centuries reminds us of how time has brought changes to the way people live. The sophisticated digital clock of today gives the precise minute at any time of the day or night, whereas the sundial could tell time only during the day, when the sun was shining and casting a shadow.

Digital clock–20th century

Watch–20th century

◄ The oldest type of writing material, used by the ancient Egyptians, is papyrus, made from reeds. The dry climate of Egypt was ideal for papyrus, but papyrus rotted in the damp European climate. As a result, parchment, the dried skin of sheep, goats or calves, came into use from the second century (100s) BC.

Four centuries later, early in the second century (100s) AD, the Chinese invented paper. This skill spread across the world extremely slowly, not reaching Italy until more than 11 centuries later, in about 1276. For a long time paper was always handmade. But in the 18th century (the 1700s), people invented paper-making machines.

A century

When is it the 20th century? Now is the 20th century, but the years are 1900s. The 1800s are the 19th century. Why is this? The century between the birth of Christ and AD 100 is called the first century on our calendar. Therefore the years 100 to 200 are called the second century. Can you work out what the years 1300 to 1400 are called?

1940 **1930** **1920** **1910** **1900**

TIME PRESERVED
MILLENNIA

With millennia we enter into ancient history. Millennia is a word which we use to mean thousands of years. A single thousand years, or 10 centuries, is known as a millennium. Some of the world's finest structures, built by different peoples at different periods during the past few millennia, still stand today.

You can still visit ancient monuments, such as Stonehenge in England and the pyramids in Egypt. The people and their civilizations are long gone, but some of their structures remain and give clues to what life may have been like in past times.

◄ The mysterious statues found on Easter Island in the southern Pacific Ocean were put up about one millennium ago. That makes them about 1,000 years old. No one knows why they were put up or by whom.

1903–the first powered flight

1885–the first petrol-powered vehicle

1712–the first steam engine, forerunner of the railway locomotive

1609–the first astronomical telescope

1900

1800

1700

1600

Travel back a millennium along the river of time and notice some of the things that have happened in each century. It's amazing to see how much has changed.

◄ The Olympic Games take place every four years. They started as a religious festival in ancient Greece in 776 BC and lasted for more than a millennium before being stopped by the Roman emperor Theodosius. The tradition was restarted by the Frenchman Baron Pierre de Coubertin in 1896, and today the games are held as a competition for athletes from all over the world.

◄ The emperor Shi Huang-di (259–210 BC) started the building of the Great Wall of China over 2,000 years (two millennia) ago. He had the wall put up to defend China's northern borders from attack by enemy tribes from central Asia. The wall, with all its branches, is 6,400 kilometres long, and if it were stretched out in a straight line, it would reach one-sixth of the way around the equator.

The Great Pyramid
The Great Pyramid was built just over 4,500 years (four and a half millennia) ago during the reign of the Egyptian pharaoh Khufu. At his death, the pharaoh was buried in a chamber deep inside the pyramid in the hope that he would have eternal life.

Stonehenge
The main structure of Stonehenge, in England, was built around 2000 BC and still, nearly 4,000 years later, nobody knows why it was made. Many people believe that Stonehenge may have been used as a giant calendar because the positions of the stones match the changing direction of sunrise and sunset and of moonrise and moonset through the year.

What are AD and BC?
You have probably noticed the abbreviations AD and BC that appear before (AD) or after (BC) written dates. These abbreviations stand for anno domini *(meaning "the year of the Lord") and "before Christ." According to the calendar most people use, our years are dated from the birth of Christ. Anything before that time goes backward into BC and anything after goes forward as AD.*

1455–the first printing press

1400s–the first watches

1300s–the first mechanical clock

1200s–the first parliament was formed

1115–the first magnetic compass

1500

1400

1300

1200

1100

1000

1522–the first ship to sail around the world

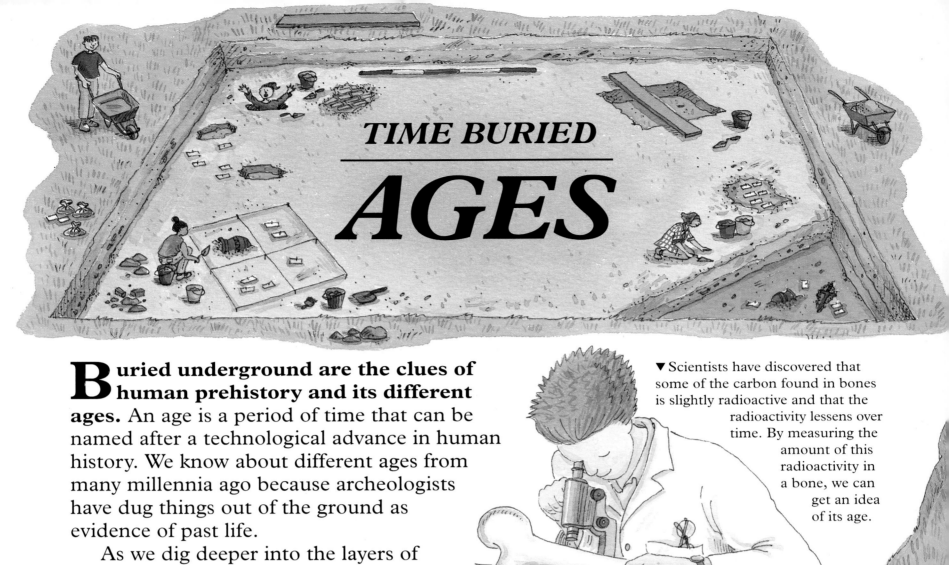

TIME BURIED
AGES

Buried underground are the clues of human prehistory and its different ages. An age is a period of time that can be named after a technological advance in human history. We know about different ages from many millennia ago because archeologists have dug things out of the ground as evidence of past life.

As we dig deeper into the layers of earth, the objects we find are usually older. In certain places, things such as shaped stones and bits of metal or pottery have been found. Archeologists classify these objects according to the periods, or ages, from which they come. Years from now, evidence of our own age may be discovered by the archeologists of the future.

▼ Scientists have discovered that some of the carbon found in bones is slightly radioactive and that the radioactivity lessens over time. By measuring the amount of this radioactivity in a bone, we can get an idea of its age.

◄ People use labels such as the "space age," the "jazz age" or the "computer age" to describe some modern periods. But these "ages" are not part of prehistory—the ages before written records that time has buried.

Evidence of different ages can be found in all sorts of places. Caves can hide wonderful Stone Age paintings.

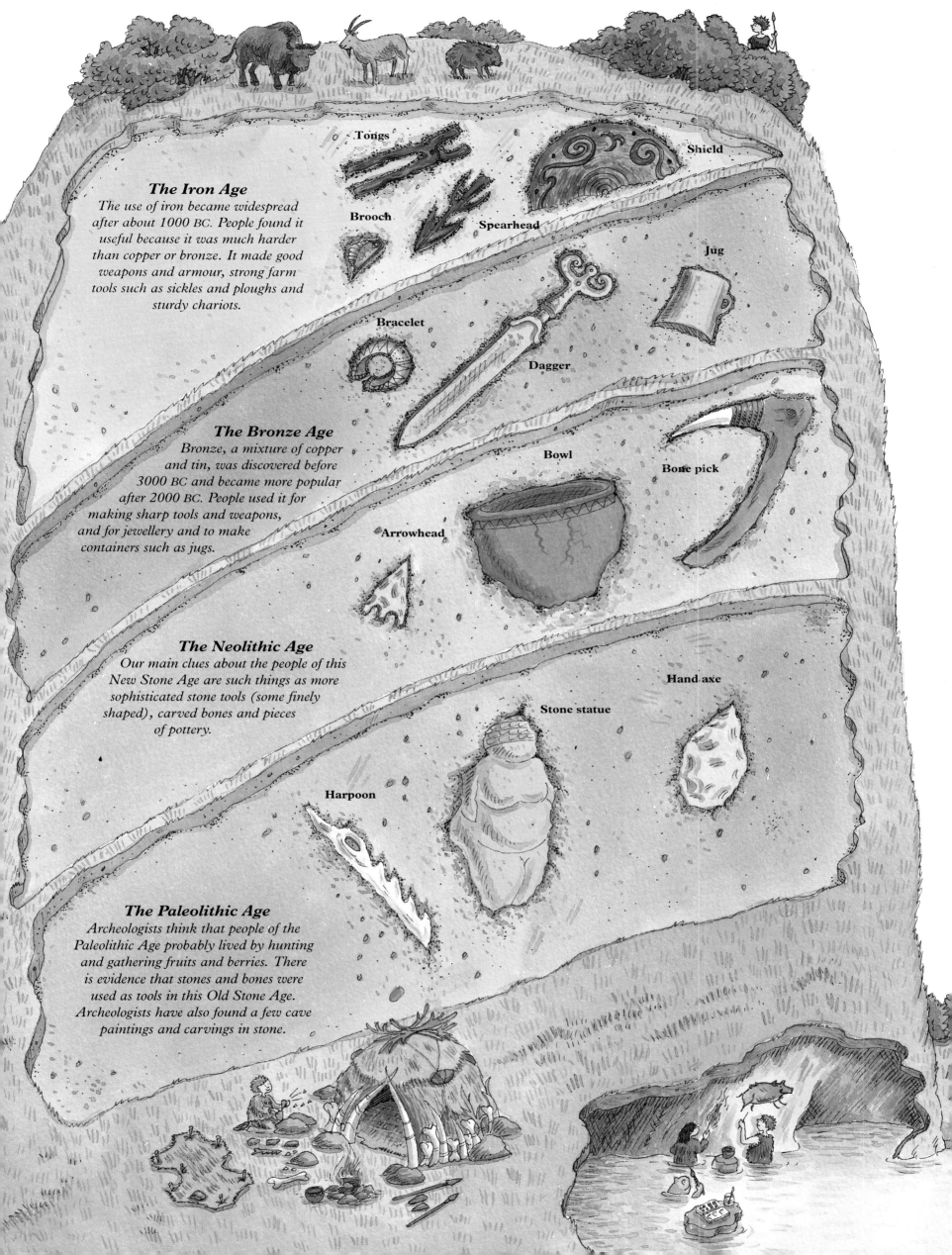

The Iron Age

The use of iron became widespread after about 1000 BC. People found it useful because it was much harder than copper or bronze. It made good weapons and armour, strong farm tools such as sickles and ploughs and sturdy chariots.

Tongs

Brooch

Spearhead

Shield

Jug

Bracelet

Dagger

The Bronze Age

Bronze, a mixture of copper and tin, was discovered before 3000 BC and became more popular after 2000 BC. People used it for making sharp tools and weapons, and for jewellery and to make containers such as jugs.

Bowl

Bone pick

Arrowhead

The Neolithic Age

Our main clues about the people of this New Stone Age are such things as more sophisticated stone tools (some finely shaped), carved bones and pieces of pottery.

Hand axe

Stone statue

Harpoon

The Paleolithic Age

Archeologists think that people of the Paleolithic Age probably lived by hunting and gathering fruits and berries. There is evidence that stones and bones were used as tools in this Old Stone Age. Archeologists have also found a few cave paintings and carvings in stone.

TIME ON EARTH
ERAS

Eras can be measured in tens of millions, hundreds of millions and thousands of millions of years. We use them to point out the stages in the whole story of our world, back to the time when our planet first appeared as a fiery molten ball. In one long era, the world cooled and crusted over, then flooded and gradually held the first signs of life in the oceans. We call this time the Precambrian Era.

After this era came three more recent eras—the Paleozoic, Mesozoic and Cenozoic. During these times, our continents slowly took shape, and an exciting, changing variety of life forms developed. All this we know from the study of rocks and of the fossils found in them. As we dig deeper into layers of rock, we find evidence of eras from longer and longer ago.

Fossil time
The ancient remains of creatures and plants that have been preserved in stone are called fossils. Geologists (people who study the earth) know to which layers of rocks the fossils belong, and so can tell in which era the creature or plant lived.

Cenozoic Era–now to about 65 million years ago.

You are here.

Paleozoic Era–about 245 million to 570 million years ago.

·Mesozoic Era–about 65 million to 245 million years ago.

36

How does a fish become a fossil?

1. A dying fish sinks to the bottom of the sea and settles on the seabed.

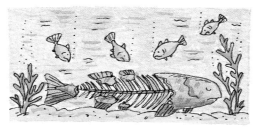

2. Slowly the fish's flesh rots away leaving only a skeleton.

3. Gradually layers of sand and soil cover the fish skeleton.

4. Over the centuries more layers pile on top and the sand becomes hard, eventually forming rock. The skeleton also hardens.

5. After millions of years the sea and land levels change, and what was the seabed is now part of the land. The rocks are eroded and the fossil becomes exposed.

Rock timing
Scientists can estimate the age of any rocks by measuring radioactivity in them. The oldest known rocks are in Canada. They have an estimated age of nearly 4,000 million years. To calculate the age of the earth, scientists have also examined lumps of rock from space that have landed on earth. All the evidence so far suggests that the earth is about 4,600 million years old.

▼ As the fiery earth cooled, all kinds of gases rose out of it. Some of these made clouds of rain, which poured down again on the earth's crusty surface, eventually covering it in an immense sea.

Red-hot time
About 4,600 million years ago our sun was born. With it came the formation of its planets, including our very own world. At first the earth was a red-hot ball of swirling molten rock. It gradually cooled and the surface hardened into a crust.

▼ The first living things were probably tiny bacteria (germs) that appeared about 4,000 million years ago. For 2,000 million years after that, at least, the only life was a kind of thin seaweed or algae. So life began as a long, long time of nothing but slime!

Precambrian Era–about 570 million to 4,600 million years ago.

LIGHT-YEARS

Beyond our world, the earth, distances are so vast that they are usually measured in time rather than kilometres. In space, the time it takes for light to travel from place to place is used to measure distances. A light-year is the distance that light will travel in one complete year. Light travels at 300,000 kilometres a second, and the speed of light is as fast as anything can go. Just think how far it travels in a year!

Using light-years as a way to measure distance, we know that the star nearest to our sun is about 4½ light-years away. When we look at a star, what we see is the light it gave out many years ago. It's like looking back in time.

38

▲ Albert Einstein (1879–1955) talked about how everything in the universe is linked together, including time and space. One way of understanding this is to think about what you say when you plan to get together with friends.

You agree on where to meet and when to meet. If you agreed only on where and not when, you could be hanging around alone all day. Likewise, if you told them when but not where, you'd never meet. Both parts are equally important.

◀ The planets came into existence thousands of millions of years ago. The dust particles swirling around the sun first fused into a huge number of rocky lumps (planetoids). These collided with each other over and over again, until they eventually formed planets, each with its own orbit.

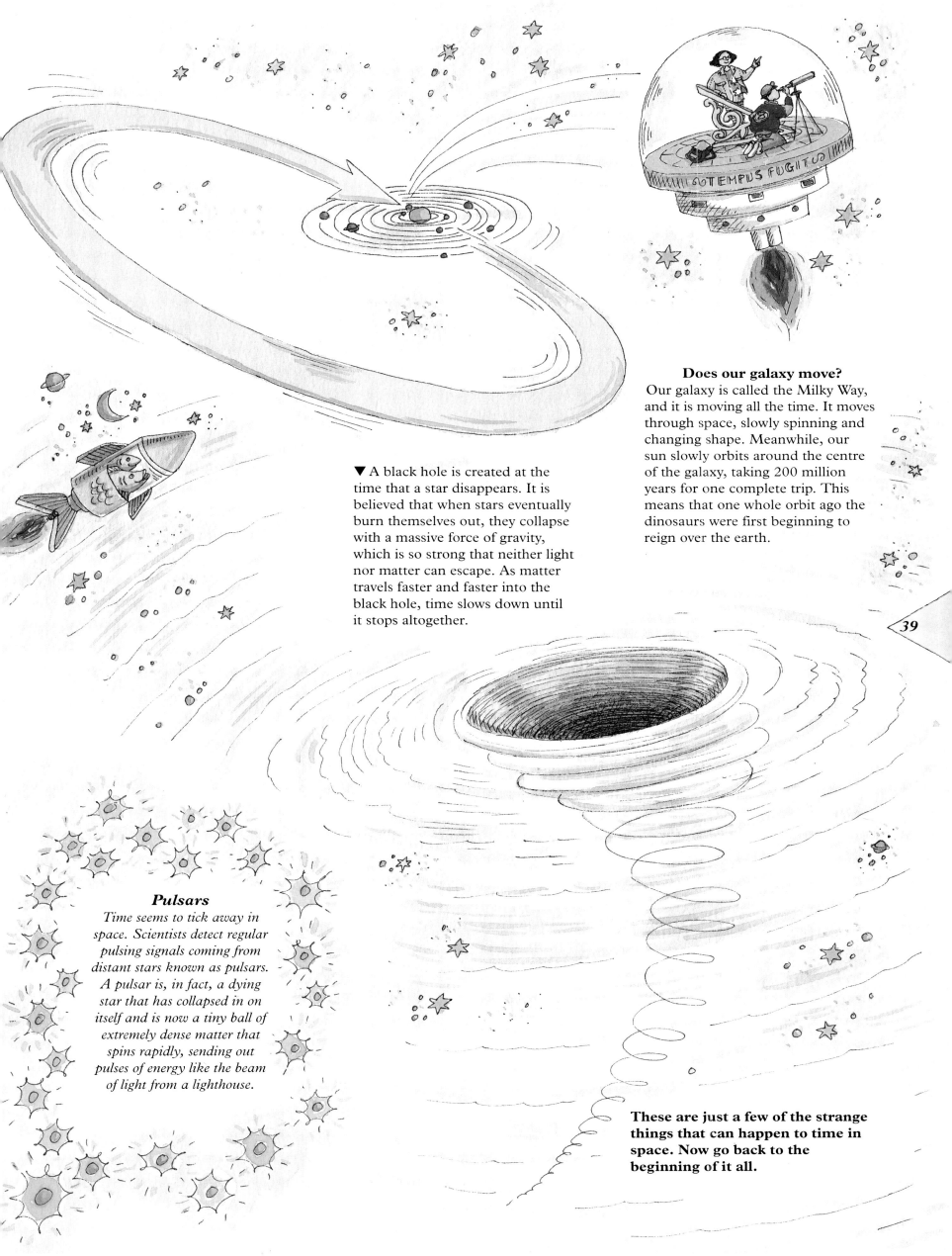

▼A black hole is created at the time that a star disappears. It is believed that when stars eventually burn themselves out, they collapse with a massive force of gravity, which is so strong that neither light nor matter can escape. As matter travels faster and faster into the black hole, time slows down until it stops altogether.

Does our galaxy move?
Our galaxy is called the Milky Way, and it is moving all the time. It moves through space, slowly spinning and changing shape. Meanwhile, our sun slowly orbits around the centre of the galaxy, taking 200 million years for one complete trip. This means that one whole orbit ago the dinosaurs were first beginning to reign over the earth.

Pulsars
Time seems to tick away in space. Scientists detect regular pulsing signals coming from distant stars known as pulsars. A pulsar is, in fact, a dying star that has collapsed in on itself and is now a tiny ball of extremely dense matter that spins rapidly, sending out pulses of energy like the beam of light from a lighthouse.

These are just a few of the strange things that can happen to time in space. Now go back to the beginning of it all.

TIME BEGUN

BANG!

Once upon a time, some people believe, there was a huge explosion that brought the universe into existence. How and why it happened are giant questions for science and religion. But much scientific evidence now seems to show that it really did happen. About 15,000 million years ago everything we know of, including time, began in this one huge explosion—the Big Bang. All our scientific rules and laws of physics, most scientists say, cannot explain what was around before then. Everything that we understand today seems to have started in the creation of one tiny speck or moment in space.

◀ Now you have travelled all the way back to the first moment of time and space. You would not be able to travel any farther back than this, if there was no time before this moment.

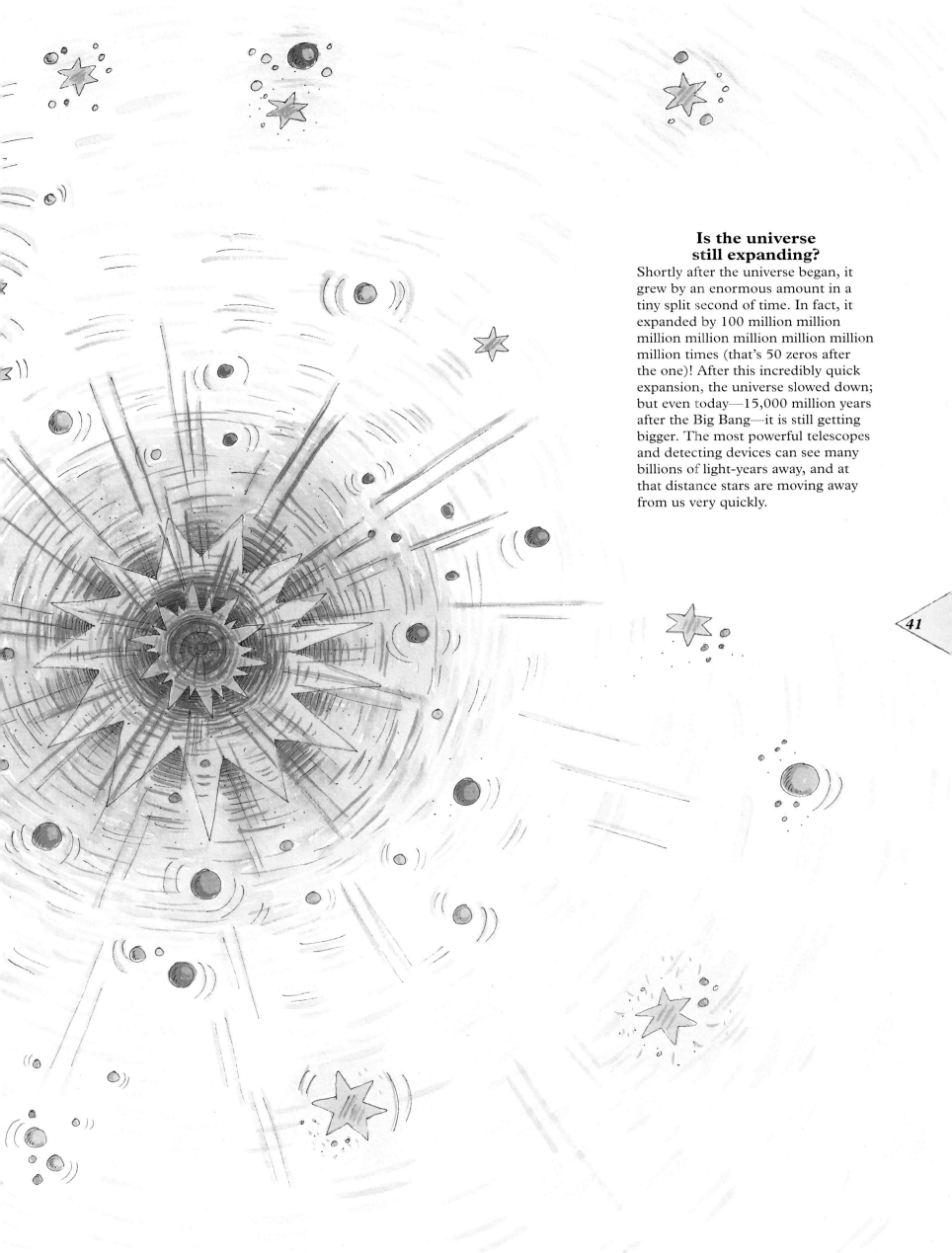

Is the universe still expanding?

Shortly after the universe began, it grew by an enormous amount in a tiny split second of time. In fact, it expanded by 100 million million million million million million million million times (that's 50 zeros after the one)! After this incredibly quick expansion, the universe slowed down; but even today—15,000 million years after the Big Bang—it is still getting bigger. The most powerful telescopes and detecting devices can see many billions of light-years away, and at that distance stars are moving away from us very quickly.

TIME TO COME

NEXT

What next? What does the future hold for us, in the next few minutes, hours, days, weeks, years, centuries or millennia? How can we know? Who can tell? There are many different people, such as fortune-tellers, prophets and scientists, who believe or have believed that they can predict the future. But nobody really knows for sure. Even so, we all like to make plans, to dream and to imagine times to come.

▲ Prophets are people—generally of times long past—believed to have received messages (often warnings) from God about the future. Ancient prophets often talked about a future life after death. This is something that can be believed in but cannot be proven.

▼ By experimenting and recording results, scientists are sometimes able to make predictions about what may happen in the future. For example, they say that the ozone layer in our atmosphere has a hole in it that is growing larger. The ozone layer protects us from many of the sun's harmful rays. Scientists predict that if we continue to use certain aerosol sprays and chemicals that damage the ozone layer, the hole will get bigger.

▲ Fortune-tellers make a business of telling people what they think is going to happen in their lives. They may look into a crystal ball, read the patterns of tea leaves at the bottom of a teacup, read the lines on people's palms or use tarot cards.

Scientists predict that the world will be a safe and good place to live only if we take care of it now. We have to be careful not to use up its forests, fuels and materials or to destroy its animals. There is plenty that all of us can do to help.

PLANT TREES

Signs of the zodiac

Taurus
April 21 to May 20

Aries
March 21 to April 20

Pisces
February 19 to March 20

Gemini
May 21 to June 21

Aquarius
January 20 to February 18

Cancer
June 22 to July 22

Capricorn
December 21 to January 19

Leo
July 23 to August 22

Sagittarius
November 22 to December 20

Astrologers studying the night sky have given names to patterns of stars or constellations. The zodiac is an imaginary band in the sky that is divided into 12 constellations, or signs. Each sign has its own dates; so if you were born on August 18, for example, your sign of the zodiac is Leo. Astrologers record the positions of the sun, stars and planets in relation to the signs of the zodiac and believe that they can tell what influence these positions have over human affairs. What is your sign?

Virgo
August 23 to September 22

Libra
September 23 to October 22

Scorpio
October 23 to November 21

Forecasting the future

People who predict what is going to happen to such things as the weather or the economy are called forecasters. Forecasters carefully study what has already happened and what is happening now. This helps them decide what is likely to happen in the future. Even so, they make mistakes and they cannot look far ahead.

How long is the future?

Will the future stretch on for another 15,000 million years and more? Or will the universe stop expanding and begin to shrink? If this happened, the galaxies would start to return to where they came from, eventually to be swallowed up in one BIG CRUNCH. That's what some scientists suggest might happen. But no one on earth really knows.

43

◀ Writers and movie makers use their imaginations to make up stories set in the future. These often include incredible machines, space travel and alien life forms. Sometimes they even tell about travelling forward in time. These stories and movies are known as science fiction.

SAVE THE PLANET

FOREVER

The great voyage of all time is now over. You have journeyed in the present, through the past and into the future. And still you are in the present. Endless time is also called forever, or infinity, that which has no limits. So what is time? Is it a river along which everything floats on and on? Or is it a wheel that brings everything around like the seasons and the days? Time is all these things and more.

44

So on and so on...

Lie back and dream about the great adventure of time. Your journey is over—but it is also just beginning, because here you are back in the present. Now is forever, because you always exist in the present—now. You now know that time is not just measured in hours, returning seasons or recorded ages. It is much, much more. You've travelled through the millennia and back to the very first moment. Time is all around, and it does not seem to end. How would you describe time to someone who hasn't been on this incredible journey?

45

The river of time winds on without stopping, through the moments and light-years of the present, the past and the future.

INDEX